THE CATHEDRAL OF
SANTIAGO DE COMPOSTELA

Text by Jesús Precedo Lafuente

© ALDEASA, 2002

© Text: Jesús Precedo Lafuente

© Photographs: Manuel González Vicente
                Imagen Mas (p. 30-31)

I.S.B.N.: 84-8003-353-3
Book catalogue number: M-9156-2002

Coordination and Production: ALDEASA
Design : Antonio Ochoa de Zabalegui
Layout : Myriam López Consalvi
Translation: Nigel Williams
Latest update: Polisemia, S.L
Photomechanical Production: Lucam
Printed in Spain by: Jomagar, S.A.

All rights reserved. The total or partial reproduction of
this book by any mechanical or photographic means is
forbidden.

Printed in Spain

CONTENTS

INTRODUCTION

FOUR SQUARES

Four squares surround the Cathedral of Santiago de Compostela. Two bear the names of craftsmen: to the north, **Azabacheros** ("the Jetworkers"), where the original name of the ancient Romanesque façade – El Paraíso ("Paradise") – was changed in the 19th Century to "La Inmaculada" as Santiago de Compostela's homage to the mystery of the Immaculate Conception, defined as a dogma of Christian faith by Pope Pius IX; to the south, **Plateros** ("the Silversmiths"); the west square (*Obradoiro*) was named after the stonecutter's workshop in which various generations of workmen interpreted with hammer and pick the mysterious language of the stonecutters; and finally, to the east, the squares of **Quintana de Muertos** and **Quintana de Vivos**, separated by a step terrace. La Quintana –**"Plaza"– de los Muertos**, today perfectly paved, was formerly a cemetery and occupies the area between the Cathedral and the Benedictine monastery of San Paio de Antealtares.

THE THIRD CATHEDRAL

Work on the Romanesque cathedral began in 1075. With time, however,

Detail from the fountain. Plaza de Platerías.
To the left: view of the Cathedral from Paseo de la Herradura.

features of successive architectural styles were added in evidence of the subsequent rectors' acceptance of the tastes of their age. Some of these new additions were completely different in style from the original Romanesque features, while others were only modifications made to the original building, as in the case of the Azabachería and Obradoiro façades.

This, Santiago's third known Cathedral, was built in the times of Bishop Diego Peláez and king Alfonso VI. Of the two earlier "known" cathedrals (for it cannot be said that there have not been others) perfectly identifiable vestiges associated with Alfonso II and Alfonso III have survived. The remains of these two churches – in no way comparable with the Cathedral as it is today – lie next to a necropolis and close to the old city walls and defence tower under the

Cathedral floor. What is left of this cemetery, which served the town throughout the first eight centuries of the Christian era, provides magnificent evidence (far fewer records exist from that period than from later times) of the settlement now known as Compostela.

THE NAME "COMPOSTELA"

The name of the cathedral's town has not always been **Santiago de Compostela**, since it was originally known as the *Lugar Santo* or "Holy Place" in clear reference to the

holy remains venerated there and was also known as *Arca Marmórica* ("Ark of Marble").

Only later was it named Santiago (after the apostle St. James in Spanish) de Compostela. Readers will often have been informed that Compostela means *Campo de la Estrella* ("Field of the Star"), but this would appear to be no more than an ingenious, rather facile invention, and is therefore probably untrue. Instead, "Compostela" would seem to refer to a piece of land or a well-tended tomb and this would certainly be as appropriate an explanation as the former.

The name *Campo de Estrella*, which is still used in the Compostela

EXTERIORS

1. THE OBRADOIRO FAÇADE

Although the tour of the Cathedral could begin at any point, for practical purposes we recommend walking around the outside first. The **Obradoiro façade** was built in the 18th century, replacing the previous Romanesque front whose features are no longer visible due to the changes made to the west-facing porch known as the Pórtico de la Gloria; this magnificent work of art, produced by Fernando de Casas y Nóvoa, was erected in response to the damage caused to the original polychrome by the ravages of time and due to a new taste for Baroque exuberance. A large number of artists collaborated with Casas y Nóvoa, including the sculptors and woodcarvers Gregorio Fernández, Antonio Vaamonde, Lens, Gambino, Nogueira, Pose, López, Ramos and Montero and the painter García Bouzas. The Baroque towers of La Carraca on the north side and Las Campanas (on which Peña de Toro collaborated) on the south were raised on top of the Romanesque towers. Striking examples of iconography on the Pórtico de la Gloria include the figures of St. James and his two disciples, Anastasius and Theodore. Next to these are the figures of

Roofing of the Cathedral. The Obradoiro Façade. Rear view. Right page: general view of the Obradoiro Façade. Pages 8-9, Plaza del Obradoiro, the Hostal de los Reyes Católicos Hotel, the Gelmírez Palace and Cathedral.

street map, would seem to refer to the celestial light that appeared to the hermit Pelayo in the 9th century. Pelayo interpreted the light that appeared above the place where he was standing as a sign from God and began to dig, subsequently reporting the great event to Alfonso II and Bishop Theodomir. Theodomir, who was still Bishop of Iria Flavia, a town 17 kilometres from Compostela, was so moved that he left instructions for his body to be buried in the town when he died. His tombstone can still be seen inside the Cathedral.

Shell on the Platerías Façade.

St. James the Less, St. Barbara, John the Evangelist and St. Susanna.

Two stairways, both dating from the 17th century, lead up from the square to the Cathedral. Beneath the steps is a church, wrongly known as the **Old Cathedral**, and built to fill the available space at a time when bringing in building materials was a costly affair. Three other buildings stand on the square. Opposite the Obradoiro façade is the **palace** named after Archbishop **Rajoy**, who ordered it built as a Consistory (Town Hall) and residence for the Cathedral confessors. It currently houses the offices of the City Council and the Presidency of the Galician Regional Government or *Xunta*. To the right, the **Colegio de San Jerónimo de Artistas** dates from the 17th century, although the 15th-century frontispiece belonged to another building that previously stood on the site. The **Royal Hospital** to the left was founded by the Catholic Monarchs for pilgrims and is now a hotel.

2. PLATERÍAS

The **Platerías façade** is the only one to have retained its Romanesque structure despite a number of modifications and

the addition of figures from other parts of the Cathedral, all of which makes it difficult to analyse. It would seem, however, to depict "The Light of the World, Jesus Christ". Certain mythological features added to the façade (possibly soon after it was built) have subsequently been reinterpreted from a Christian standpoint. The main figure is Christ the King accompanied by saints and with Abraham at his feet, admiring his descendant. The figure at the bottom may be Moses, as suggested by the horns used to represent this figure in reference to the light that illuminated his face after his meeting with God. The scene also contains the

Plaza de Platerías. Cathedral Façade and the Los Caballos fountain. Left: the Platerías façade. The Creation of Adam.

figures of five apostles, two of which are damaged and cannot be identified; the other three are St. John, St. Peter and St. James. The latter is identified by a Latin inscription on the figure's halo: *Iacobus Zebedei*. He is flanked by the trunks of two trees, which may be cypresses. To his right stands the monarch who commissioned the construction of the present Cathedral and who is also identified by an inscription: "Alfonso Rey". It is worth drawing special attention to the statue of David playing the rebec on the left-hand side of the entrance. The left tympanum displays the Temptations of Christ, while the right is divided into two parts, the upper depicting the Adoration of the Magi and the lower scenes from the Passion.

The original work on this façade is attributed to Bernardo and Roberto.

3. THE CLOCK TOWER

The Plateresque construction on the left was designed by Rodrigo Gil de Hontañón and dates from the 16th century. The echeloned tower at the southern end is known as the **Torre del Tesoro** ("Tower of the Treasure") since it holds ornaments and other objects of worship. It seems

Clock face, which unusually has only one hand, to mark the hour, on the tower of the same name.
Previous page: details from the Platerías façade. Figure of David (left), Christ in Majesty (right) and tympanum (bottom).

given its slender shape it was named after Queen Berenguela. The Baroque section was built by Domingo Antonio de Andrade in the 17th century. The present clock mechanism was made by Antelo in Ferrol in the 19th century. The clock faces display the hour hand only and two recently restored bells chime the quarter-hour and the hour.

4. QUINTANA AND PUERTA SANTA

The eastern square of the Cathedral is called **La Quintana**, which means Plaza or Square. The upper part is known as "Los Vivos" ("The Quick") and the larger, lower area as "Los Muertos" ("The Dead"). For a long time it was a cemetery. The large section of wall directly opposite the Cathedral belongs to the Benedictine Convent of St. Pelayo (or San Paio) de Antealtares, previously a monastery closely linked to the cult of St. James in which the Benedictine monks alternated with the Cathedral canons. Nine sections, some circular and others polygonal, were added to the Cathedral's large apse. However, as time passed yet more new constructions were built, some for worship, others for defence and offices, all of which upset the original structural harmony. As a result, in the 17th century the Cathedral Chapter

that its shape, reminiscent of Chinese architecture, is imbued with influences from the Americas. Some writers, however, consider that this kind of tower is a homage to Divine Motherhood. Another tower, which stands closer to the Fonseca building, is known as the Torre de la Vela.

To the right, the **Clock Tower** is a mixture of Gothic and Baroque. The first section, which is cube-shaped, is Gothic and was built in the 14th century on the instructions of Archbishop Rodrigo del Padrón. Its name – La Berenguela – may be due to the fact that it was fortified by Archbishop Berenguel de Landoira in order to defend himself from the attacks of the Compostela bourgeoisie. Another theory, however, holds that

decided to remodel the area through a project designed by Vega y Verdugo and implemented by José de la Peña. Of the three doors on this façade, the most striking is the Puerta Real ("Royal Door") on the far left. Also known as Puerta Quintana ("the Quintana Door"), on All Souls' Day – 2 November – the Chapter comes to the door in procession to pray for the dead buried in La Quintana. Built between 1658 and 1661, its inner face is thought to be Compostela's first Baroque work.

The **Puerta Santa** ("Holy Door"), which is the second to the right, is only opened during the "Holy" or "Jubilee" Year in Compostela, an ancient rite that dates from the 12th Century and which is celebrated whenever the Apostle's feast day – 25 July – falls on a Sunday. This takes place in a sequence of 6, 5, 6, and 11 years. The first Holy Year in this century will be 2004. In accordance with an ancient ceremony, the Door is opened on the afternoon of 31 December of years previous to "Holy Years" and is closed on the evening of the following 31 December. A small Romanesque door inside is one of the nine with which the Cathedral was originally endowed. The façade dates from the 17th century. The twenty-four small statues adorning it depict apostles and

prophets and came from the stone choir carved by Master Mateo. The three larger statues of St. James the Pilgrim and his two disciples – Anastasius and Theodore – above the façade were produced by Pedro Docampo in 1694.

5. THE AZABACHERIA FAÇADE

To the left of the Quintana stairs is the Parish Church of La Corticela, built as an oratory possibly in the 9th century. It was attended by the monks of San Paio even after they had built the Monastery of San Martín Pinario. It is now a parish church for foreign pilgrims.

The **Azabachería façade** takes its name from the jetworkers' guild, to which the street leading into the Cathedral's north square was dedicated. According to the Codex Calixtinus, which is the first guide that existed of the *Camino de Santiago* (the pilgrim's route to Santiago de Compostela), its old name was *Paraíso* ("Paradise") deriving from the stories told by its Romanesque sculptures. Here the French route to Santiago ended. The first example of Compostela Neo-Classicism, this

façade was built by Ventura Rodríguez, Luca Ferro Caaveiro and Clemente Fernández Sarela, among others. Ferro and Fernández began the work but due to certain discrepancies Domingo Lois Monteagudo, who had studied under Ventura Rodríguez, was commissioned to continue the work, although he may actually have only made changes to the iconography. The statue of Faith was produced by Gambino; the statues of St James the Pilgrim, Alfonso III and Ordoño II and the portraits of Charles III and his wife Maria Amalia of Saxony are the work of Máximo Salazar.

THE INTERIOR OF THE CATHEDRAL

1. THE SANCTUARY

The Cathedral can be entered through this door
Visitors should first stop to view the **high altar**, above the Apostle's tomb. Constructed in Baroque style under the supervision of Canon Vega y Verdugo, it erased all traces of the Romanesque work, which had already been modified in the 15th and 16th centuries. Although the ciborium or canopy had to be adapted to the available space, hence its

Side panels flanking the Puerta Santa with figures of the Apostles and Prophets.

disproportionate shape, it retains its great beauty. This work was performed by Domingo Antonio de Andrade. Other artists also worked on the **sanctuary**: the masters Francisco de Antas and Bernardo Cabrera; the Flemish marble workers Gutier, Sameria and Broces; the sculptors Pedro del Valle and Mateo de Prado, responsible for most of the sculpture work; and various woodcarvers from Compostela.

The High Altar contains three images of St. James. The one at the bottom, from Mateo's workshop, is the image of St. James the Teacher; the next one is of St. James the Pilgrim, and the third is of St James the Knight (by Mateo de Prado). It is worth highlighting these three superimposed depictions of St. James: in the chamber he is St. James the Doctor, seated and receiving the pilgrims in his chamber; above it he is St. James the Missionary, preacher of the faith; on the baldachin he is St. James the Warrior, defender of the Christians during the Reconquest and in other battles. Paying homage to St. James are four Spanish kings closely associated with devotion to the saint: Alfonso II, Ramiro I, Ferdinand V and Philip IV. At the four corners are statues representing the Cardinal Virtues: Prudence, Justice, Fortitude and Temperance.

The **choir stalls** were made when the old choir at the centre of the

Cathedral was removed. They were designed by Martínez Pidal and Pons Sorolla and built by Del Río in 1949. Of the lamps, three are of special interest: the lamp on the right was donated by María I; the lamp on the left by Archbishop Monroy; and the one in the centre by Canon Diego Juan de Ulloa.

The **high altar** was remade by Constenla in 1879. The silver was donated by Archbishop Antonio de Monroy (who was born in Querétaro, Mexico) and sent to Spain from his homeland. With this silver Antonio de Montaos made the frontal and the steps, and Juan de Figueroa the tabernacle and the display cabinet. The image of the Immaculate Conception, designed by Manuel de Prado, was carved by the sculptor Francisco Pecul.

The two **pulpits** were made by the Aragonese Juan Bautista de Celma. The left pulpit reproduces scenes from Antonio de Arfe's monstrance, while the one on the right displays scenes on the theme of St James as the protector of all Spain. Both were produced by this artist in 1583. Miguel Romay made the canopies in 1714.

Two alms boxes are attached to the pulpits. The one on the right dates from 1527 and stands at the foot of a stone image of St. Salome, who was St. James's mother and a relative of the Virgin Mary's. The one on the left dates from 1497 and displays an image of St. James the Less, son of Alphaeus.

Pulpit and image of
St. James the
Apostle on the High
Altar.
Following page:
general view of the
High Altar.

2. THE APOSTLE'S CHAMBER

Pilgrims may approach and embrace the polychrome stone seated image of St. James the Teacher, made by the school of Master Mateo. Archbishop Monroy donated the cape and the staff, both made by Figueroa. Without doubt the custom of embracing the Apostle had much to do with the pilgrim's joy when, having fulfilled his obligations (including the confession of his sins), he came like the prodigal son in the gospel to be reconciled with the father of all Spaniards in the faith. It is said that before the halo was added to the

statue, pilgrims placed their hats on the Apostle's head in order to embrace him more easily. Above the pilgrim's head is the votive lamp made from the silver hilts of weapons donated by Fernández de Córdoba, *El Gran Capitán* (the "Great Captain"), in 1512 when he came to Compostela as a pilgrim.

3. THE BURIAL CRYPT

The **tomb of St. James** and his two disciples **Anastasius and Theodore** should be visited next. Visitors often wonder how the body of an apostle of Christ came to rest in a place as remote

To the left: detail from the Choir; to the right: alms box with the image of St. Mary Salome.

as Finisterre. According to tradition, St. James actually preached in these parts. If this is true and these testimonies preceded the rediscovery of the tomb in the 9th century (after a period of relative oblivion), it is not difficult to accept that the Apostle was indeed buried in Compostela. The crypt is situated at the end of a cemetery used between the 1st and 8th centuries and facing the Quintana de Muertos.

After this period of relative neglect, which ended in the 9th century during the time of Bishop Theodomir and Alfonso II, the Apostle's remains were not hidden again until the period between the

time of the Englishman Drake's incursion in the 16th century and 29th January 1879. The successive alterations made to this area now make it impossible to determine its precise appearance in antiquity, although sufficient remains exist to give a general idea. It was indeed a Roman construction dating from the 1st and 2nd centuries and similar to other constructions unearthed elsewhere. It had two chambers: a lower chamber, the tomb itself; and an upper chamber that served as an oratory and a meeting place. Historically, it is important to bear in mind the subsequent structures, the

Muslim invasion and the alterations made to the site, particularly in the 12th and 17th centuries.

Work on the crypt as it is today began in 1879, following the line adopted by the historian and Cathedral Canon López Ferreiro. Every effort was made to evoke the old adornment. In July 1884 the silver casket containing the three bodies (recomposed and classified at that time by professors from the Santiago de Compostela Faculty of Medicine), each in a different compartment, was placed in position. It stands on the original burial site, albeit in a higher position, since the current crypt lies at the same level

as the upper section of the Roman construction. Designed by Losada, the casket was made by the local silversmiths Rey and Martínez in imitation of the altarpiece (dating from the time of Archbishop Gelmírez), which stood behind the altar in the 12th century. The lid displays the Christogram – the symbol of the Greek name of Christ in the form of an X and a P, which correspond to J and R. Depicted on the front and sides are the Saviour, flanked by ovals or almonds, and the apostles beneath arches. The rock crystal cross on the altar was donated by Archbishop Gaspar de Zúñiga y Avellaneda in 1569.

Tomb of St. James the Apostle with depictions of the Saviour and the Apostles.

Mass before the
tomb.
Following page:
central nave with
the Baroque organs.

4. THE PÓRTICO
DE LA GLORIA

Towards the Portico

The Pórtico de la Gloria can now be reached by walking down the central aisle. Together with the westernmost structure, which was lost when the Obradoiro façade was built, it was exposed to the elements, with the subsequent deterioration of the paintwork and even the stonework. On the way to the Pórtico de la Gloria visitors can admire the lamps and organs but must look upwards to marvel at the Gothic **dome**, completed in 1445, and which rises to a height of 32 metres. The corners display the arms of Archbishop Lope de Mendoza, during whose pontificate the dome was

completed. The balcony around the inner face dates from the 17th century and José de la Peña de Toro was commissioned with the ornamentation. Made in Vizcaya in 1602, the system of pulleys used for the *botafumeiro* or incense burner (discussed later) was devised by Juan Bautista de Celma.

The first lamp on the way to the Pórtico de la Gloria came from the Senate and was donated by Montero Ríos, a local resident. This is followed by two organs, both dating from the 18th century, and which can be played from the same console. They are supported by columns from the 17th-century choir. The cases were made by Manuel de la Viña between 1704 and 1712 and their Baroque adornments were produced by Miguel Romay between 1705-1712. When the choir stood at the centre of the nave it formed, together with the **organs** and the sanctuary, a continuous display of 17th-Century art. The **lamp** was displayed at the Paris International Exhibition of 1855. Its decorative elements include acanthus leaves, branches, filaments and rock crystal. Donated by Canon Pedro Méndez Acuña, it was offered to the Cathedral in his name by relatives.

Information on the Pórtico de la Gloria

It is said that when Ferdinand II visited Compostela in the 12th

Dome.
Pages 30-31:
complete view of
the Portico de la
Gloria.

century, the west side of the cathedral was either unfinished or in poor condition, and that the king decided to leave his palace architect, Mateo, behind in Santiago with sufficient funds to finish the work that can now be admired. This was confirmed in a document in which Ferdinand II granted Master Mateo "one hundred *morabetinos* (ancient coins among the Arabs)" of gold per year "for all the time of his life so that the work on the Cathedral may be attended to with zeal". The name of the author also appears on the Portico itself, the central arch of which contains an inscription that reads as follows:

"In the year of the Incarnation of the Lord, 1188, in the era 1226, and on the first day of April, the lintels of the main porch of the Church of Blessed St. James were placed in position by Master Mateo, who directed the work [on the Cathedral] from [the time of the laying of] its foundations".

This took place at the time when the so-called "Beati" codices were being copied from the manuscript of Beatus of Liébana, who in the 8th century had made commentaries on the Book of Revelation, all of which brought this last book of the Holy Scriptures into vogue and prompted the appearance of the

famous miniatures of the new school led by Magius. Indeed the Pórtico de la Gloria clearly displays the influence of the Book of Revelation.

Since it was not customary to keep a record of the architectural work carried out on the Cathedral, there is no official description of the Pórtico de la Gloria. We can therefore only speculate on the meaning conveyed by this "book" carved in the polychrome stone and which, like sculptures and paintings in any church, was intended to enlighten the faithful on the mysteries of the faith. The most probable hypothesis is that the Pórtico de la Gloria depicts two of the most important aspects of the Church: the Militant and Triumphant.

Nothing is known about **Mateo**, although there are theories on certain homonymous contemporaries of his who may have been either the master himself or some relative. Some accounts refer to him as a Galician but others, referring to certain influences evident in his art, claim that he came from beyond the Pyrenees. However, there is no doubt as to his skill, which is so wonderfully reflected in this work. Is the orant statue facing the altar a self-portrait? It may well be. The posture reflects piety, humility

Dome above the Portico (left) and keystone of the upper part of the Portico.

and thankfulness to God. This figure is known as Santo dos Croques.

Christ, the Apostles and the Prophets

St. Paul wrote on redemption in his epistle to the Ephesians: "Ye are fellow-citizens with the saints, and of the household of God; and are built upon the foundation of the apostles and prophets". In his work, it is quite clear that Mateo bore the doctrine contained in these words carefully in mind. The main figure (almost three metres tall) on the Pórtico de la Gloria is Christ, seated and revealing the glorious wounds in his hands.

He is accompanied by the four evangelists, two on each side, their symbols making them easily identifiable: St. Mark with the lion, St. Luke with the ox and St. John with the eagle, although St. Matthew appears without the angel. On the lower part of the arch, angels carry instruments associated with the Passion. On the upper part are twenty-four seated figures carrying musical instruments. They represent the twenty-four elders described in the Revelation of St. John; "And round about the throne ...... I saw four and twenty elders sitting, clothed in white; and they had on their heads crowns of gold" (Revelation 4:4).

One of the most interesting musical instruments that they are holding is the "organistrum", with its strings and sounding wheel. The small images beneath these (miniatures used to depict a crowd) represent the faithful who have already gone to heaven.

The figures on the right are apostles; beginning from the inside, they are Peter, Paul, James and his brother, John the Evangelist, while those on the left are Prophets, representing, in the same order as the apostles, Moses, Isaiah, Daniel and Jeremiah. The monstrous creatures on the bases are reminiscent of the hybrid guardians found in Assyrian and Babylonian palaces and may represent the vices crushed by the Church. The figure at the centre that is prising open the mouths of two lions with his hands may represent the Celestial Father, Creator of the Universe.

Jews and Gentiles

In the Bible, mankind is divided into two groups: Jews – members of the people of Israel, into whose number Christ was born – and gentiles.

Here are also the two divisions of mankind called to form part of the Church. On the right, between the central and side arches, are naked figures, one of which an angel covers

To the left: the trumpeter angel who, in the Gospel according to St. Matthew, will announce the Last Judgement; and to the right: St. James the Apostle on the mullion.

with a cloak in a symbol of baptism and grace. On the left, also naked, are the representatives of the Jews, bearing a cartouche recalling the books of the Old Testament – the Jewish Scriptures.

The arch on the right displays strange animals gripping men in their claws. These clearly represent the vices, which enslave mankind. On the left arch are three archivolts adorned with foliage and a number of human figures. These represent mankind awaiting the coming of the Messiah. On the lower archivolt, Adam and Eve see God's Messenger, who has come to free the universe from their sin.

The Prophet Daniel. To the right: detail of one of Jesse's patriarchs, David, on the central column of the mullion.

The Christological Column

In the middle of the central arch and beneath the seated figure of St. James the Great (who is holding a tau staff and a cartouche with the inscription "the Lord sent me") is a white porphyry column that offers a lesson in Christology, for here artistic representations of the human and divine origin of Christ come together. The human aspect is seen on the shaft in the form of a tree sprouting from the chest of an elder who is lying on the ground – almost certainly David's father, Jesse. Among the branches are a number of figures, two of which are clearly distinguishable: David, holding a musical instrument; and Solomon, with the royal sceptre in his right hand. Above the tree top and free of the branches is the Virgin Mary. The fact that she is not touching the branches may be a reference to belief in the Compostela church, even as early as the 12th century, in the mystery of the Immaculate Conception – which was not to be defined as a dogma until the 19th century.

The capital displays the Holy Trinity, i.e. the divinity of Christ, through customary iconography: the Father is a crowned elder with the Son upon his knee. The Holy Spirit is symbolized by a dove, recalling the

passage in the gospel on the baptism of Christ, in which it is written, "And Jesus, when he was baptised, went up straightway out of the water: and lo, the heavens were opened unto him, and he saw the Spirit of God descending like a dove and lighting upon him." The dove and fire are images used in the Holy Scriptures to symbolize the Holy Spirit, undoubtedly to emphasise the fire of the love that the Holy Spirit kindles in the hearts of men and the purity instilled by his gifts.

Santo dos Croques

Traditionally this Galician name is given to the kneeling figure behind the trumeau of the Pórtico de la Gloria and facing the high altar. A cartouche clutched in his hand bears the inscription "Architectus". The figure is believed to be a self-portrait of Master Mateo. The story goes that the Portico's master mason had used his

own likeness for one of the figures on the inner face and that the Archbishop reproached him for his effrontery in including himself among the representatives of the Church Triumphant when he was no more than a member of the Church Militant. The master then decided to render himself in this humble and thankful posture. If "croque" is a Galician word, then it means "a blow, either given by or received on the head" and pilgrims usually bring their heads close to that of the statue in the hope of receiving some of Mateo's inspiration. According to other theories, "croque" comes from an Occitan, Provençal or Limousin word meaning "curl", which would make the figure "the Curly-haired Saint".

In addition to the popular rite of butting master Mateo's head, pilgrims also insert their fingers in the spaces between the branches of the tree in the central column. Although it is said that the pilgrim will thus receive as many mercies as there are fingers on both hands, the church authorities make no claim of this nature.

Top: the Santo dos Croques *on the central column of the Portico.*
Right: space between the branches of the tree where pilgrims place their fingers believing they will receive as many mercies as there are fingers on both hands.

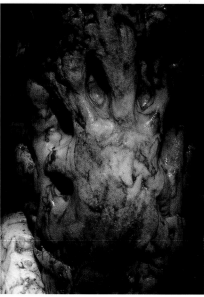

5. THE RADIATING CHAPELS

Towards the Ambulatory

A door on the south side-aisle towards the east end leads to the Relics Chapel

and St. Ferdinand's Chapel (now the Treasury, discussed later). The first door on the south transept leads to the **Sacristy** (not open to the public). This door is a beautiful plateresque work built, together with the Cloister door, by the architect Juan de Álava in 1527. The portrait of La Virgen de Guadalupe to the right was donated by the Santuario Nacional de México. The Sacristy formed part of the construction work on the Relics Chapel in the 16th century and contains 25 paintings on copper: the twelve in the lower section are 18th-century Flemish paintings depicting the

12 articles of the Creed, each attributed to an apostle, while the remaining 13 depict scenes from the life of Christ and the Virgin Mary. The Sacristy also contains canvases by Gregorio Ferro, Juan Antonio Bouzas and Modesto Brocos. Next to the Sacristy, the **Tympanum of Clavijo**, originating from the cloister commissioned by archbishop Gelmírez, depicts the moment in which the maidens thank St. James for releasing them from their forfeiture. The legend of how the apostle St. James appeared to the Asturian king Ramiro I and aided him against the Muslim troops of the Emir of Cordoba, Abd ar-Rahman II, at the Battle of Clavijo, is told in the "Privilegio de los Votos" of 1150. This document also refers to the one hundred maidens paid in tribute each

year since the times of the Gothic king Rodrigo (710-711) and Mauregato (783-789) by the kingdom of Asturias to the Muslim king of Cordoba. With this victory Ramiro I abolished payment of the tribute.

The stoup in the opposite corner is believed to have come from the 9th-century church and is said to have been used by Almanzor to water his horse. Above appear a Castilian group of sculptures dating from the 16th Century, and which flank the exit to Plaza de la Quintana. Next to this, on the façade of the Chapel of Our Lady of the Pillar, is the tomb of the bishop of Iria Flavia at the time of the reencounter of the relics of the Apostle in the 9th century. The Latin inscription reads: "In memory of the bishop of the Iria Flavia See. Teodomiro found the

tomb of the Apostle St. James and founded the City".

The construction of the **Chapel of Our Lady of the Pillar** was financed by Archbishop Antonio de Monroy in the 17th century. The mausoleum containing his remains is surmounted with an orant statue carved by Fernández de Sande. The chapel displays the work of two Baroque master masons, Andrade and Casas. The dome is octagonal and the marble altarpiece was designed by Casas and built by Romay. The stone image of Our Lady of the Pillar was brought from Saragossa, while the other figures were made by Sande, who used fossilised shells to adorn the Apostle's cape.

Built in the Flamboyant style, the next chapel has two names: The

Pietà Chapel, due to its advocation; and The **Mondragón** Chapel, after its founder, Canon Juan Ibáñez de Mondragón, who lived in the 16th century. The site may correspond

The Puerta Santa ("Holy Door") from inside the cathedral.

to that formerly occupied by the old San Pelayo door. It was built in the Flamboyant Gothic style in 1525 by Jácome García. The Pietà, or Descent from the Cross, is made from baked clay, although some say that it is pumice from Vesuvius. The next chapel, which has three names – **St. Peter**'s, **La Azucena** and El Magistral (referring to the fact that its patron is the canon who holds this position) – was founded by Mencía de Andrade in 1571. The Baroque altarpiece was designed by Fernando de Casas and built by Francisco das Moas. The image of St. Judas Thaddaeus is deeply venerated as the patron of desperate cases.

The "Puerta Santa" and the Saviour Chapel

The **"Puerta Santa"** ("Holy Door") or "Door of Forgiveness" (although this name is commonly given to facade which leads up to it) is one of the seven minor doors mentioned in the Codex Calixtinus, the first guide to the Pilgrim Route to Santiago, written in the 12th century on the orders of Pope Calixtus II. It is flanked by two polychrome stone sculptures made in Master Mateo's workshop. In the cartouches to either side of the door, a Latin inscription reads, "All the nations shall come and say: Glory to Thee, O Lord."

The **Saviour Chapel** was the first to be built; indeed, the work on the current cathedral began with the construction of this chapel in 1075. It retains its original architectural and ornamental layout; the capitals display the first examples of Romanesque art in the cathedral. It was consecrated by Bishop Gelmírez in 1102. Inscriptions on the two capitals at the entrance inform visitors that work began in the times of Bishop Diego Peláez and Alfonso VI. A similar inscription was also carved on the walls, but most of it was destroyed when the niches were built. On this site Archbishop Alonso de Fonseca established the "Compostela Office", which issued certificates to the effect that pilgrims had completed their pilgrimage; the certificate is still issued today, providing the pilgrim has completed the route and brings a signed statement to this effect. Also stationed here were the priests known as *lenguajeros* who confessed pilgrims in their own language before they attended Holy Communion and were issued with their official certificates.

The polychrome stone altar was designed by Juan de Álava and financed by Archbishop Alonso III de Fonseca (16th century) and two saintly bishops of Compostela – Rosendo and Pedro de Mezonzo (to whom the Salve is attributed). The Fonseca arms, which

Altar belonging to the Saviour Chapel.

Altar of the Chapel of Our Lady of the Snows. To the right: the Virgin of Walsingham in the Chapel of the same name.

displays five stars, recalls the generosity of a member of this family in providing the ornamentation of this chapel, which in all other respects has remained unchanged since its Romanesque construction.

The chapel is also known as both the **French Chapel** – as Charles V the Wise of France established a foundation in 1380 for the celebration of holy mass in the chapel and – when

Louis XI endorsed the foundation in the 15th century – the **St. Louis King of France Chapel**.

The chapel opposite (and directly behind the high altar) formerly served as the sacristy, a confessional and the "Compostela Issuing Office" until Alfonso III had these functions transferred to the Saviour Chapel. At that time it was known as both the **Confession Chapel** and the **Mary Magdalene Chapel**, in honour of this woman who was a model penitent. There is another image of Mary Magdalene on the altar in the Saviour Chapel. The altarpiece, which was made by Pedro de Valle in 1671, displays three scenes from the life of St. James the Great: his martyrdom; the transference of his remains; and his burial. The star that surmounts the Apostle's mausoleum can be seen between the altar and the altarpiece. In front of the altar is the spot where in 1589 Archbishop Juan de Sanclemente ordered the Apostle's remains hidden so that they would not be plundered by the Englishman Drake.

From the Our Lady of the Snows Chapel to the Holy Spirit Chapel. Dedicated to the Virgin Mary, the next chapel is known both as the **Our Lady of the Snows Chapel** and the **España Chapel** after its patrons, the España family, some of whose members (with others from the Torrado and Arousa families) are buried here. According to an inscription on the lowered 16th century arch over the entrance, the Chapel was founded in the late-14th or early-15th century by Juan Miguélez de Camiño and completed with funds provided by Fernán González do Preguntoiro. A cross was reinstalled at the time of the chapel's consecration dating from 1211.

Due to the Romanesque walls of the adjacent chapels, it has an irregular pentagonal shape. It has a vault of irregular ribs that is supported by columns adorned with plant motifs. The Neo-Gothic altar was made by Magariños in the 20th century. The

image of Our Lady was made by Gregorio Fernández in 1747. The two other images – Our Lady of Walsingham (English) and Our Lady of Montserrat (Catalan) – date from the latter half of this century. The Brotherhood of St. Eligius, patron saint of silversmiths, was founded in this chapel.

In the 16th century, Jácome García made alterations to the **Chapel**

The St. John the Apostle Chapel.

Top: altar in the
St. John the Apostle
Chapel. Bottom:
tomb of Canon
Diego de Castilla
in the
St. Bartholomew
Chapel.

of St. John the Apostle and
St. Susanna (co-patron of the city of
Santiago de Compostela). The chapel
was named after the Baroque
altarpiece images of St. John
(15th century) and St. Susanna, carved
by Mariñas in 1902, although for
centuries it was known as the Parish
Church of St. John the Apostle. The

image of St. Dominic of the Way,
donated by the Ministry of Public
Works in the Holy Year of 1965, was
made by Frechilla.

The name of the original
Chapel of Santa Fe de Conques was
changed to that of **Our Lady of Good
Counsel** and **St Bartholomew**. It was
originally dedicated to the Virgin

Mary only but when Canon Gómez Rodríguez de Sotomayor established the foundation of St. Bartholomew in 1516, Bartholomew's name was added. Particularly interesting are the capitals. The small Plateresque altarpiece is the work of the Flemish woodcarver Mateo Arnao, who also carved the Coimbra marble tomb of Peter the Cruel's great-grandson, Canon Diego de Castilla (d. 1521).

There are two entrances to the Chapel of the **Immaculate Conception**. The original entrance is to the left, and led to the old apsidal chapel of the Holy Cross. In 1525, the Brotherhood of the Prima Clerics (this room is also known as the **Prima Chapel**) was granted permission to enlarge its cathedral headquarters and dedicate an altar to the Immaculate Conception. The extension work was performed by Master Jácome García, according to the plans of Juan de Álava, in 1525. The stone image of Our Lady of O was produced by Cornelis of Holland in the 16th century and was repainted and bejewelled in the 18th. It offers a curious example of the iconographic image of the Virgin Mary, since the Child that she holds in her arm is holding a cross, which immediately links Christ's death with his birth. The Descent from the Cross was carved by Diego Fernández de Sande in 1721,

Top: view of the Chapel of the Immaculate Conception; and to the left: image of the Immaculate Conception in the chapel of the same name.

while all the other figures were made by Antonio Alfonsín and Manuel de Leis. Virtually indistinguishable on the floor is the tomb of the Baroque master mason Domingo Antonio de Andrade.

Since the 13th century the site of one of the Cathedral's original doors, that of St. Mary, has been occupied by the **Holy Spirit Chapel**. This was founded by Pedro Vidal, who provided an endowment for matins to be said in it by twelve chaplains. These chaplains were known as Sancti Spiritus Chaplains until the middle of the 15th century, when Archbishop Álvaro Núñez de Isorna founded a college for them and appointed them *Racioneros de Sancti Spiritus*. There, on a corbel,

appears a painting of La Dolorosa ("Mary of the Sorrows"), produced by the painter Marius in 1872. The chapel was enlarged in the 14th century and further alterations were required in the 16th and 17th centuries. The altar and the image of Our Lady of Solitude, originally in the retrochoir, were transferred to the chapel in 1945. The image of the Virgin Mary was made in Madrid in 1666. The embroidered mantle was donated by Archbishop Rafael de Vélez in the 19th century. The silver altar and steps were made in the 18th century by Antonio Morales and the pedestal, the angels and the ornaments were made by Francisco Rodríguez. The Calvary dates from the 15th century.

Image of Santiago Matamoros *("St. James the Moor-Slayer"), produced by Gambino in the 18th Century.*

A Parish Church for Foreign and Basque Pilgrims

At this point a staircase leads up to the Parish Church of **La Corticela**. This is known to be one of the oldest churches in Santiago de Compostela, for as early as the 9th century it was an oratory, which depended on the nearby Benedictine monastery. When the Benedictine order built the Church of St. Martin and its oratory, the monks continued to attend La Corticela from time to time in order to retain entitlement to certain rights connected with it. Although the current building is the result of work carried out between the 11th and early-13th century, it was restored in the middle of the 20th century. It was founded in the Middle Ages as a parish church for foreign and Basque pilgrims, once staffed by priests known as *lenguajeros* who confessed pilgrims in their own languages. Romanesque like the rest of the church, the frontispiece displays an Adoration of the Magi, a very common motif in Compostela as the three kings who came to adore Christ were pilgrims as well as representatives of different peoples, all of which underlines the universal nature of pilgrimage to Santiago de Compostela. Our Lady of Consolation presides over the church. The Christ Child of Prague was the patron of the Tecelanes. The jetworkers' guild also once had an image of their patron, St. Stephen, here. The cults of the "Prayer of Jesus in the Garden" and "Our Lady of the Miraculous Medal" are also extremely popular in this church although their iconography does not match the architectural purity of this building, which was not originally connected to the Cathedral.

To the right, the chapel dedicated to **St. Andrew** was the seat of the parish of the same name previously situated in the area now occupied by the Our Lady of the

Pillar Chapel. The side altars are dedicated to Our Lady of Mount Carmel and to St. Joseph. In a niche, an image of Our Lady of Luján, donated by the Doello-Teruelos, replaced an earlier one brought to the church by Eva Perón. The chapel was built in the 17th century.

6. THE CHAPELS ON THE NORTH SIDE-AISLE

From St Anthony's Chapel to the Christ of Burgos Chapel
St. Anthony's Chapel, which took over the functions of St. Nicholas's Chapel when it was demolished to make way for the Church of La Corticela, was once also the parish see of St. Fructuosus (now in the old Church of Las Angustias de Abajo). The altarpiece dates from the 18th century. The image of Our Lady of Fátima was brought to the chapel from the Portuguese village in 1948. On the right wall hangs a painting of the Virgin of Czestochowa, a gift donated by a Polish citizen to commemorate the two visits of His Holiness John Paul II to Compostela.

The next chapel after the Azabachería entrance is **St. Catherine's Chapel**, dedicated to the saint of Alexandria and built before the 16th century. This chapel contains a

St. Catherine's Chapel.

reproduction of the apparitions of the Virgin Mary in Lourdes.

The image of **St. James the Knight** was made by Gambino in the latter half of the 18th century. This depiction of St. James represents the Apostle's protection of the Spanish nation over the centuries and is based on the tradition of his appearance to Ramiro I at the Battle of Clavijo (actually fought by Ordoño I). It is displayed on a door, which once led to the next chapel, that of **Lope de Mendoza**, named after its founder, who was Archbishop of Santiago de

Del Río and Nogueira. Made by Lens, the altarpiece was originally situated in the Relics Chapel. The statues of four doctors of the Church in niches were carved by Gregorio Español and Juan Vila. In the 16th and 17th centuries university degrees were awarded here. Archbishops Mendoza and Rajoy are buried in this chapel. The construction of the **Christ of Burgos** or **Carrillo Chapel** was ordered by another archbishop, Pedro Carrillo y Acuña. Built in 1665 by Melchor de Velasco y Agüero, it stands on a Greek cross plan and has a coffered dome. A copy of the original, the fine image of Christ was carved in Burgos in 1754. The Baroque side altars, made by Melchor de Prado, display two scenes from the gospel: the intercession of St. Salome on behalf of her children, on the right; and St. Peter weeping after his denial of Christ, on the left. The tombs at the sides are of Archbishops Carrillo and García Cuesta, while the one in the floor is of Zacarías Martínez Núñez, another Archbishop of Santiago.

THE MUSEUMS

After concluding the tour of the Cathedral interior, the next rooms to be visited are the Museums, two of which are inside the Cathedral and one (discussed later) outside.

The Communion Chapel. Following page: Christ of Burgos and bust of Santiago el Alfeo (St. James the Less).

Compostela from 1399 to 1445, and which is also known as the **Communion Chapel** and the **Sacred Heart Chapel**. To the right of the entrance, the Archbishop kneels at the feet of the alabaster image of Our Lady of Forgiveness begging for God's mercy through her intercession. The present chapel, a Neo-Classical rotunda with a dome, was built in the 18th century on the orders of Archbishop Rajoy; it was designed by Ferro Caaveiro and constructed by

1. THE RELICS CHAPEL AND THE TREASURY

After the visit to the Chapel of the Christ of Burgos or the Chapel of Carrillo, visitors must then pass through three naves and head towards the door opposite that leads to the Relics Chapel and the Chapel of St. Ferdinand.

The **Relics Chapel** was designed by Juan de Álava and was built between 1521 and 1529. In 1921 Fernando Cabrera's altarpiece and with it almost all the images made by Gregorio Español were destroyed by fire. In 1925 Maximino Magariños made a new cedarwood altarpiece to a design by Rafael de la Torre.

The one hundred and forty relics venerated in this area are contained in urns, busts, glass cases and images. Particularly important is the head of St. James the Less. It contains a silver bust with an enamelled face – donated by Archbishop Berenguel de Landoira in the 14th century – and bedecked with a necklace donated by Suero de Quiñones in the 15th century. Also important is a 13th-14th century image of St. James the Great donated by the Parisian Coquatriz and containing a bone. This chapel also contains the head of St. Pauline, brought from Cologne by Archbishop Gaspar de Ábalos in 1544. The silver bust with an enamelled face was

Bust of St. Pauline.
Bottom, image of
St. Teresa and
image of
St. James the
Pilgrim.

produced by Jorge Cerdeira (1533). Finally, a 19th-century image of St. Teresa of Jesus contains one of the saint of Avila's teeth and her signature.

The many other objects displayed in this chapel include a reproduction of a cross donated by Alfonso III in 874; a 16th-century Italian rock crystal and gold pax donated by Charles II in 1638; silver cornucopias adorned with precious stones and biblical motifs; a small alabaster altarpiece donated by the English priest Gudgar in 1456; a chalice and paten said to have belonged to St. Rudesind; and a silver-gilt St. James the Pilgrim sent to the Cathedral from Paris by Juan de Roucel and his wife in the 15th century.

The royal tombs were transferred here from St. Catherine's Chapel in 1535. The tombs on the right contain the remains of Ferdinand II of León (whose recumbent statue may have been made by Mateo), Alfonso IX, Conde Traba and Don Pedro Froilaz; on the left are the tombs of Doña Berenguela, wife of Alfonso VII, Conde Ramón de Borgoña, Alfonso's father, and Juana de Castro, wife of king Peter I of Castile.

The vestibule contains various paintings by Cancela dating from the 19th century, one depicting the appearance of the Virgin Mary to St. Felix of Catalicio and attributed to Murillo, as well as the tomb stone of Bishop Theodomir, who died in 847.

It was during Theodomir's pontificate that the remains of St James the Great were rediscovered, prompting the bishop's wish to be buried close to the Apostle's tomb rather than in the capital of his see, Iria Flavia (situated between Compostela and Padrón).

For almost one hundred years, during the 16th and 17th centuries, **St. Ferdinand's Chapel** was used as the Relics Chapel. It was named after Ferdinand III the saint, who called himself "the standard bearer of St. James". Ferdinand accompanied his father, Alfonso IX, at the consecration of the cathedral in 1211, and, as king in 1232, returned to Compostela as a pilgrim. His image, on the altar, was carved by Seoane in 1676. The frescoes of the Ascension of Christ and the Assumption of the Virgin were painted in 1540.

The silver-gilt monstrance was made by Antonio de Arfe in the 16th century. Below it are six reliefs with scenes from the life of St James, beginning with his calling by Jesus and ending with the transference of his remains; one other scene depicts the miracle of the hanged man and the resuscitated cockerel as told in the Codex Calixtinus. Twenty-four smaller reliefs depict scenes from the life of Christ. Homage is also paid to the Eucharist through four figures of doctors of the Church. The coral image of St. Christopher on a silver and bronze background is Italian and is said to have been donated to the Cathedral by John of Austria. The jet image of St James was made by E. Mayer in 1919. The silver cup, which is used in the "Ofrenda Nacional" or "National Offering" ceremony, was donated by the Duke of Montpensier and his wife, Isabella II's sister. The hammer is one of those used to open the Holy Door. The chapel also contains: shell-shaped trays (the

Monstrance of St. Ferdinand's Chapel.

scallop-shell is traditionally associated with St James); various chalices, paxes and other liturgical objects; a pair of rock crystal candelabra; a crucifix with gold mountings, also of rock crystal (the figure of Christ is also of gold); a display cabinet with the hat of Cardinal Quiroga Palacios, who died in 1971; and a triptych donated to the cardinal by the authorities of his province of origin, Orense. The last monstrance is adorned with jewels donated by the Ferreiro de la Maza family. Both it and the triptych from Orense were made in the workshop of Ángel Iglesias.

Among the ornaments are 16th-century copes and 18th-century chasubles and dalmatics.

2. THE CLOISTER

The **cloister** can be reached either through the **Museum** entrance from the Relics Chapel and Treasury or through the Museum from the Obradoiro square. The present cloister is the third that has existed at the Cathedral: the first, dating from the times of Gelmírez, was perhaps completed by Master Mateo; the second dates from the 13th Century; and the present cloister

General view of the Cloister.

was built between 1521 and 1590. This is a Castilian Gothic style work with Renaissance influences. The cresting is extremely beautiful. The fascia with Romanesque ornamentation curves to accommodate the coats of arms of the great patrons of this work – Archbishops Fonseca, Taaber and Sanclemente. At the centre of the courtyard stands a large stone basin from the Azabachería façade; it originally belonged to the fountain at the "Paradise" door mentioned in the Codex Calixtinus. The three sun dials on the arches date from 1601.

The Dawn Chapel.

The initiative of the project came from Archbishop Alonso III of Fonseca, with the collaboration of Juan de Álava, Jácome García, Rodrigo Gil de Hontañón, Juan de Herrera and Gaspar de Arce. The door that leads to the Relics Chapel was reopened in 2001.

3. THE DAWN CHAPEL AND THE ARCHIVES

The **Dawn Chapel** stands at the end of the north cloister close to the Museum. It was founded in 1529 by Canon Gómez Vallo so that mass could be celebrated there each day at daybreak, hence the chapel's name. The 18th-century altarpiece, which replaced one made previously by Cornelis of Holland, displays the scene of the Transfiguration.

On the southwest corner of the cloisters are the **Chapter Archives**, which contain extremely important documents relevant not only to the Cathedral but also to the whole of Galicia; some, such as those referring to the "Voto de Santiago" ("Santiago Offering"), are relevant to an even greater geographical area. Particularly valuable are the Codex Calixtinus, Registers A, B, C and D, which contain records dating from the 9th to the 14th century, and original diplomas, etc. The Archives are open to researchers.

4. THE LIBRARY AND THE CHAPTER HOUSE

On the west side of the cloisters are two rooms. The first is the **Chapter Library**. Its collections were generously dontated by Canons Pedro de Acuña Malvar and Diego Juan de Ulloa. It was built by Ferro Caaveiro and Arias Varela in the 18th century. The movable pulpit dates from the same period. Particularly interesting are the frescoes and sanguines on the ceiling and frieze depicting the life, martyrdom and miracles of St. James the Great. At the corners are portraits of Doctors of the Church. The themes depicted in the medallions above the doors and the paintings on the west wall are Abraham's sacrifice of Isaac, the Queen of Sheba's visit to Solomon and the flagellation of St. Roch.

To the left are two *botafumeiros* or incense burners. The first was donated by the "Brotherhood of Provisional Standard-bearers" in 1971, while the second was made in 1851. The *botafumeiro* is known to have existed as early as the 14th century and must originally have been used to add more solemnity to religious occasions and also to freshen the air in the Cathedral at those times of the year when it was filled day and night

View of the Archives.

Different scenes depicting the tiraboleiros *and the* botafumeiro *produced by Losada in 1851 to replace the one taken by the French in1809. Following page: Library interior.*

with travel-stained pilgrims. It weighs 54 kilos.

The *botafumeiro* is used before mass, when the archbishop leads a procession, on important feast days and for certain pilgrimages to the Cathedral. During processions it is used to cense the presiding relic. Eight men known as *tiraboleiros*, (a Galician form of the Latin thuribularii) pull on the lower ropes that are fastened to the cable and swing the burner in the direction of the transepts of the crossing, forming a 50-metre arc, and almost touching the vaults; the burner is said to have broken free on various occasions, although there have never

been any casualties. One such occasion was in 1501, in the presence of Princess Catherine, who was on her way to England to marry Arthur, Prince of Wales, and another was in 1662. On other occasions onlookers who came too close received a few scratches and bruises.

The next room is the **Chapter House**, so named because it is the official meeting place of the cathedral canons, who form the "Chapter" (from the Latin "Capitulum" meaning "a meeting of canons"). The old Chapter House and Library were destroyed in a fire in 1751. The new buildings were raised by the architect

The Chapter House.

Lucas Ferro Caaveiro, a pupil and successor of the master builder Casas y Nóvoa, whose influence is evident in the architecture of this room, although it was actually designed by Luca Ferro Caaveiro. The granite vault was stuccoed and gilded by Aguiar. The frontal was made by Bartolomé Sernini, who worked on the Royal Palace of Madrid; the St James the Pilgrim is by Gambino; the canopy, made at the Royal Tapestry Factory of Madrid, was designed by Guillermo de Anglois for Charles III's bed-chamber. Also made at the Royal Factory, the other tapestries (some of which are Flemish) were woven from cartoons by Teniers and depict scenes from the lives of Achilles and Scipio. Also of interest are the 18th-century brazier with motifs alluding to St. James and two cases made of lignum vitae inlaid with mother-of-pearl and ivory. The painting of Our Lady of Guadalupe was donated by Archbishop Antonio de Monroy, who was born in Mexico.

5. THE CATHEDRAL MUSEUMS

The Cathedral Museums consist of three main areas, each with a ticket

office. They are the Treasury (the door is located in the central nave to the left), the Crypt beneath the Pórtico de la Gloria, and the Archaeological and Tapestry Museums (access via the Plaza de España entrance to the right of the Obradoiro façade). In the following brief descriptions of their contents, the Archaeological and Tapestry Museums will be discussed first.

Ground Floor. Archaeological Museum and historical part of the Cathedral

This floor consists of four rooms, the last of which displays new exhibits recovered from part of the work of master Mateo.

The first room exhibits items unearthed in excavations carried out over various centuries. They date from the 1st to the 10th century and illustrate circumstances surrounding the Apostle's tomb. Also exhibited are items from the two churches – raised by Alfonso II and Alfonso III in the 9th century – which existed before the present Cathedral was built. Furthermore, on pieces such as the Setecoros and Carcacía capitals (which come from sites close to the first diocesan see, Iria Flavia) there are illustrations of

View of the corredor that circles the Tapestry Museum.

Tympanum depicting the Adoration of the Magi, dating from the 14th century.

early Christianity in this region of Galicia.

The second room is dedicated to the current Cathedral, built on the orders of Alfonso VI. The items are divided into two groups according to their dates. The first group covers the time of Bernardo the Elder (1075-1088) and includes moulds from the original capitals, while the second (1100-1165) covers the time of master Esteban and his work on the Platerías façade (the only work by this builder and his school to have survived), and consists of marble shafts and depictions of Adam and Eve, the month of February, and Christ in Majesty.

The third room covers the period (1165-1211) when master Mateo and his assistants completed their work. In 1211 the Cathedral was consecrated for the last time. The items corresponding to this period include an arch, rose windows, imposts with angels, sculptures and capitals. Also exhibited is a 17th-century drawing of the west end by Canon Vega y Verdugo.

In the fourth room outstanding features include a mile-stone of Caligula to the left dating from 40 A.D., and to the right the rose window originating from the exterior facade of the portico replaced by the current baroque style façade. The rose

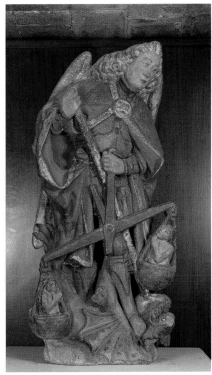

Virgen de la
Esperanza *or
de la* O *(left),*
St. Michael the
Archangel consoling
souls *(right).*

window was produced in Mateo's
workshop, together with various choir
stall pieces. At the end are various
materials unearthed during excavation
work performed in the basement of
the Cathedral after 1946. Leaving this
room to the right visitors come to
another room that contains a perfect
reconstruction of the choir of Mateo,
produced by professors Otero Túñez
and Izquierdo Perrín, whose design
was used for the reproduction and
funded by the Pedro Barrié de la Maza
Foundation. At the entrance is a
model that reproduces the design of
the aforementioned professors, as well
as a glass-covered section of the
Roman road that ran through this

place, known as *rúa de Valladares*. A
video shows the reconstruction work,
which was completed in July of the
Compostela Holy Year of 1999.

The mezzanine. Sculptures and paintings

The first room displays items dating
from the 13th to 16th century, the
most important being the following:
an anonymous 15th-century wood
and alabaster altarpiece dedicated to
St. James and named after its donor,
the English priest Gudgar; a
tympanum depicting the entrance
of Jesus into Jerusalem; a 13th-century
seated image of St. James; a
14th-century tympanum depicting

Body of St. James on Queen Lupa's ox cart. Polychromed wood. Archaeological Museum. Following page: Top: reconstruction of the stone Choir of Master Mateo. Bottom: detail of a dossel and horses from the entourage of the Magi (the Epiphany) in the choir.

the Adoration of the Magi; a 16th-century Christ Crucified by Celma; Our Lady of Expectation (also known as Our Lady of O); the Archangel Gabriel, from the 15th century; and The Three Generations (Anne, Mary and the Child), which are in the Hispanic-Flemish style.

The second room contains sculptures dating from the 13th to 19th century, the most important being reliefs by Gregorio Español depicting the life of St. James (from the altarpiece in the Relics Chapel before it was destroyed by fire).

The third room has recently been dedicated to Numismatics (coins and medals) and important documents belonging to St. James. On display are

coins unearthed during the excavations, a wide range of coins produced in the Compostela area, as well as coins from different countries and brought by pilgrims in the Holy Year of 1976.

Upper floor. Tapestries
The first room contains tapestries by Teniers, Ginés de Aguirre and Castillo. The largest, depicting the Holy Family asking hunters for food, is by Castillo. All were made at the Royal Tapestry Factory in Madrid. There are also two items of Cordoban leather. The pennant (17.5 metres in length) from the flagship at the Battle of Lepanto was donated by John of Austria in 1571.

The second room contains tapestries depicting scenes from the story of Achilles and other mythological themes. The cartoons were produced by Rubens and Van Thulden at the workshops of Jan Raëz and Erasmus Oorlofs in Brussels. The chest for holding ornaments dates from the 18th century. This room also contains a small alabaster altarpiece, a gift from the English priest J. Goodyear in 1456 and which

Tapestry depicting scenes from the life of Achilles based on cartoons by Rubens.

images, including a polychrome terracotta Our Lady Nursing the Child made by the sculptress Roldán (better known as "La Roldana"), copper kitchen items, a silver bowl and a giant candleholder.

The fourth room contains tapestries from cartoons by Bayeu and González Ruiz. The pig-slaughtering scene dates from Teniers's blue period and was made at Melter's workshop in Lille.

The fifth room exhibits tapestries made from cartoons by Goya and donated by Charles IV to his Foreign Secretary, Pedro de Acuña, canon of the Cathedral. All were made at the Santa Bárbara Royal Tapestry Factory. The pictures were painted in the 17th century by Gregorio Ferro, dating from the 18th century, the Compostela artist who was appointed Director of the Royal Academy of San Fernando in preference to Goya.

represents five scenes of life, martyrdom and the transference of the remains of St. James the Apostle.

The third room contains tapestries (at the top) with scenes of rural life made at the Royal Tapestry Factory in Madrid from cartoons by Teniers. The Game of Skittles, however, apparently came from Melter's workshop in Lille, and the beggar may have been painted by Antonio González Ruiz. In addition to the tapestries there are paxes and

6. THE CRYPT BENEATH THE PORTICO

Before entering the Cathedral and viewing the items displayed in the Treasury, visitors can also take time to visit what is wrongly known as the Old Cathedral. Lying beneath the main staircase, at the same level as the square, this area is in fact no more than

a crypt made by Master Mateo to compensate for the unevenness of the ground and to enable subsequent construction work on this three-storey structure. Believed by many to have been built by Archbishop Gelmírez and completed by Mateo, the Crypt appears to date from the late-11th century. Another theory holds that it was built entirely by Master Mateo around 1168. However, Romanesque elements in the early-Gothic structure have prompted the theory that Mateo did not actually build the Crypt but only made alterations to it. It was dedicated to the worship of the apostle St. James the Less or *Santiago Alfeo*. The bosses of the ribbed vaults display an angel with laws, by Mateo, and the moon, by master Ropas Mojadas, who also made a number of pieces on the Crypt's old frontispiece.

Also admirable are the reproductions of the musical instruments held by the elders on the Pórtico de la Gloria; this work was

View of the Crypt of the Old Cathedral.

Double-nave lower room.

financed by the Barrié de la Maza Foundation and studied by professor López Calo.

THE GELMÍREZ PALACE

The **Gelmírez Palace**, recently associated with the cathedral Museum, is named after the first Archbishop of Compostela, Diego Gelmírez, who decided to build this to replace the residence that had suffered severe damage during the serious revolts of 1117. However, most of the work on the present Archiepiscopal Palace was carried out by other Archbishops, such as Juan Arias in the 13th century, Lope de Mendoza in the 15th century, Alonso III of Fonseca in the 16th century, and Maximilian of Austria in the 17th century. The latter was also responsible for designing the outer wall that looks onto Plaza de España (Obradoiro). The masters who contributed successively to the work were Pedro Bonet and Fadrique. The latter produced the panelled room, which no longer exists, and which was painted by Francisco López.

In terms of the Palace, two floors and the remains of a third have been conserved, as well as the tower staircase. The two floors form a T. The lower floor, dating from the 12th century, is almost twenty metres long by eight and a half metres wide. It is formed by two galleries divided into five sections; the vaults consist in groins supported by semicircular arches on four columns with decorative floral capitals.

The staircase to the second floor, which also leads up to the tower, takes visitors to the Romanesque kitchen, with its barrel-shaped vault. Next to the kitchen is a small room that may have been the quarters of the tower guards. To the right are the remains of the Gothic work, incorporated into the offices of the archiepiscopal curia, and not open to the public. Further along the left is the large room that

was used as a dining room and scene of large festive celebrations.

This room must have been completed by the time of archbishop Juan Arias, i.e. the 13th century. It is thirty-one metres and ninety centimetres long and eight and a half metres wide, with a height, up to the keystones of the arches, of six metres and ten centimetres. It has six ornamental Gothic vaults, the last of which is split by two arches supported on cylindrical-shaft columns, partially hiding the original decorations, of which three figures arm in arm are visible. The first sections have galleries that project outwards.

Special attention must be drawn to the thirteen elaborate corbels, which depict scenes of the age. According to one theory, these may have been inspired by the wedding of Alfonso IX of León, since the banquet is presided by a king and queen: in the first section, the corbel shows a priest blessing the food of the banquet; the second presents a couple eating pastry and the servants carrying bread and wine vessels; the third depicts musicians, ever-present at the celebrations of the age; the couple reappear in the fourth, attended by servants; the fifth shows the king and queen joining the musicians, playing the *zanfona* (type of hurdy-gurdy),

Upper room.

Corbels in the dining room on the upper floor. Guests. Bottom: tomb of Teodomir, founder of the city and discoverer of the apostle's tomb.

the so-called "organistrum"; the king is again present in the sixth, accompanied by musicians; the seventh shows the person responsible for reading during the meal; the eighth presents an angel with a phylactery or tape with inscriptions; in the ninth, next to the king and queen, who are eating, appear a reader and a juggler who are making a bear dance; the angels in the tenth are carrying phylacteries containing two Latin maxims with the following inscription: "the faithful male will be crowned in heaven" and "do not do to others what you do not like yourself", the golden rule of charity; the king and queen reappear as musicians in the eleventh; in the twelfth, five servants bring the necessary hand-cleaning items; and in the thirteenth, the chief taster gives his verdict on the food, represented in this case by the pastry.

Archbishop Gelmírez commissioned the construction of his private chapel in this palace dedicated to St. Paul the Apostle, St. Gregory, St. Benedict and St. Anthony. The Palace also housed the Mint; king Alfonso VI ordered Gelmírez to perform coining work there in order to used the subsequent profits to subsidise the completion of the work on the Cathedral.

This book, published by Aldeasa, was printed on
18 October 2002 in Madrid at the printing facilities of
Gráficas Jomagar.